£2

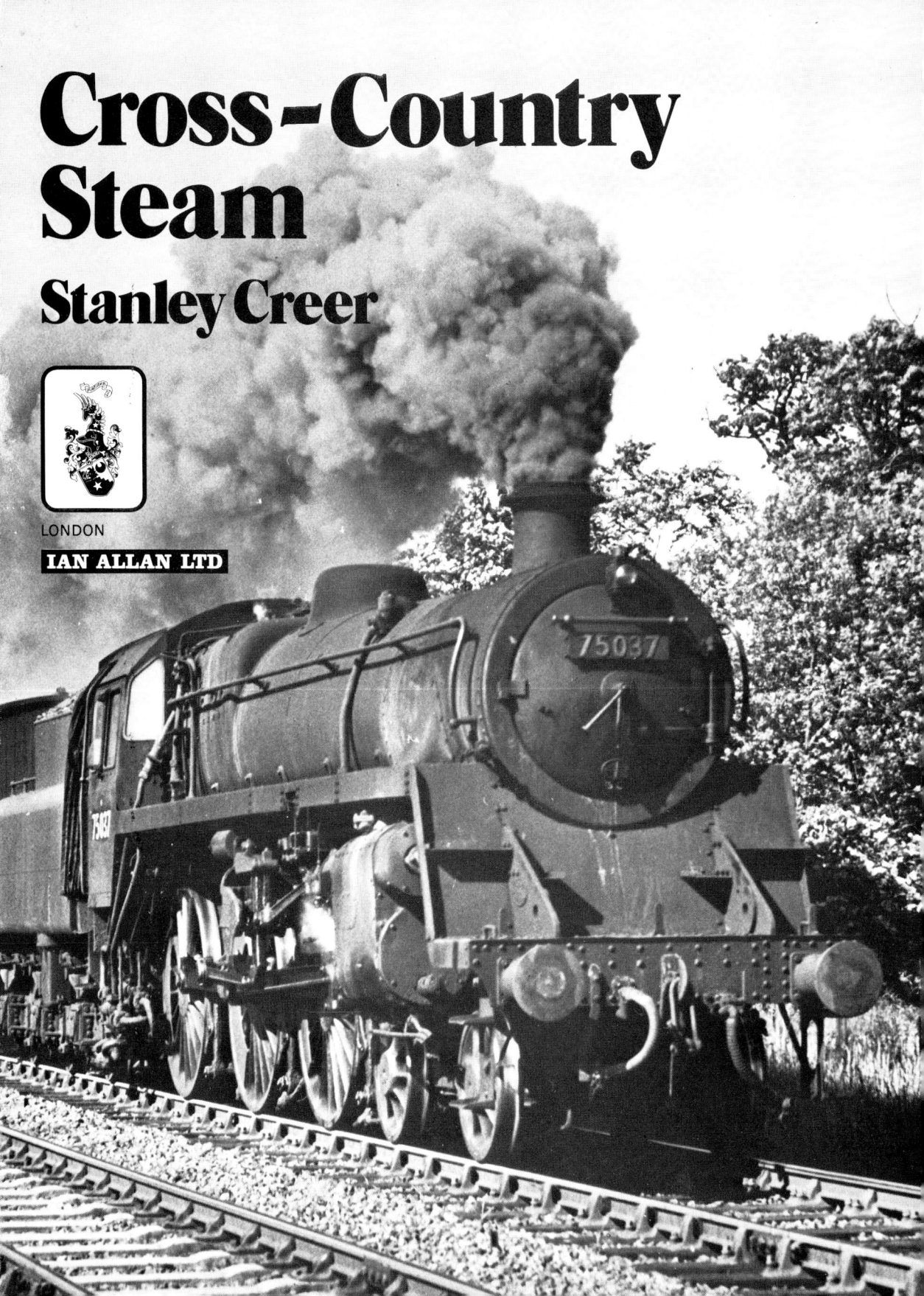

Cross-Country Steam

Stanley Creer

LONDON

IAN ALLAN LTD

First published 1979

ISBN 0 7110 0928 7

© Ian Allan Ltd 1979

Published by Ian Allan Ltd, Shepperton, Surrey;
and printed in the United Kingdom by
Ian Allan Printing Ltd

Introduction

Cross-country services have always been the Cinderella of the timetable; it seems that when the natives elect to travel by rail it is to head north or south, rarely to deviate in any other direction. To go east or west or diagonally to lesser known destinations you have to change though today this exercise is, in far too many cases, more easily said than done because the replacement bus service has followed the train into limbo. It was possible at one time to travel in a through coach from Southampton to Glasgow via the Didcot, Newbury & Southampton Railway route, an example of how a cross-country journey could be made with a minimum of effort; or a customer could reach Oxford in a through carriage from North Wales detached from a London train at Bletchley. What pleasure the timetable student can derive from his specialist interest in tracing the routes followed on such occasions; what a feast also for enthusiasts at the lineside at that period with through workings providing opportunities to see locomotives from other companies at work.

The Midland & South Western Junction line also provided facilities for through coaches from far flung outposts; now both systems are but a memory as is the Somerset & Dorset Joint Railway, of all cross-country routes, perhaps, the most glamorous. Thus a great many of the lines and services recorded in these pages have disappeared for ever. The Beeching plan — a polemic of the time — was particularly biased where holiday season traffic was concerned; some of the proposals for its curtailment were implemented in no uncertain manner when closure of the Midland & Great Northern Joint Railway was effected in 1959.

In the nature of things, cross-country trains, one supposes, were something of an anathema to the operating people; many traversed single track, always

Left: Fowler Class 3P 2-6-2T No 40011 was one of the few members of the class to travel north of the Border; it is seen here working the Craigellachie to Boat of Garten service for which it had been earmarked. Some few months later No 40011 made way for what was hoped would be the salvation of ailing branch lines — the railbus — but all to no avail. Closure of the line came in October 1965. The photograph shows the train approaching Ballindalloch station in July 1958. / *D. M. C. Hepburne-Scott*

3

a hazard to punctuality, creating problems where a main line had to be joined or sometimes crossed; or a station platform had to be occupied when it needed to be free. The dice was loaded against cross-country lines with such awkward characteristics, which hastened their end, not forgetting that other factor which is ultimate in deciding a line's future — revenue.

It is agreeable to note that cross-country routes still have an important role in the British Rail network. However, despite reassuring statements from ministerial quarters that no further retraction is envisaged, there is no room for complacency. Remarkably the Central Wales Line still lives on, massively buttressed by grant aid and the object of some effective publicity. The Newcastle to Carlisle link has the advantage of a steady freight flow, and the North East/South West route has benefited from increased investment. But there are still many services requiring reappraisal in order to improve speeds, connections and rolling stock. Other passenger services continue to face uncertainty as, for instance, along the south coast and between Tonbridge and Reading.

As has been noted, many of the services have disappeared; conversely, however, many of the locomotives which worked the trains have had representatives of their class rescued from the scrap heap and restored. Indicative of the strength of feeling for the steam locomotive is the fact that of the 92 classes shown in the following pages considerably more than half have been so favoured.

Ranging from Scotland to Dorset, all these photographs are evocative of many happy hours at the lineside or on the platform, to the individual reader some more so than others depending on where his favourite location tended to be. One scene in particular brought back to me most vividly a pleasant day spent in the vicinity of Woodford Halse some years before its demise. This is M. Mitchell's photograph of Class 4F 0-6-0 No 44524 crossing the Great Central main line south of the station. It recalls the day when with my good friend George Grimsey, I stood at what looks to have been the identical spot and watched another locomotive of the same class (it might even have been the same one) making somewhat slow progress up the hill, the fresh breeze wafting the smoke from the chimney in exactly the same way as seen in

the picture. I can still hear the measured beat of that exhaust. Happy days indeed!

The emphasis in the book is on through routes; purists may cavil at the inclusion of a few branch lines, but this is deliberate; they appear for their interest and they do, after all, go across the country.

For railway enthusiasts, railwayists, 'gricers' (awful word) — label us how you will — the hobby has been the means by which an above-average knowledge of geography has accrued. I recall with some satisfaction an occasion when, years ago as a new recruit in the service of the Postmaster General, my interest in railways enabled me to give, without any hesitation, the answer to a query from a seasoned colleague. When sorting mail the odd letter is encountered insufficiently addressed, usually with the county missing, in which case, if the town is unfamiliar to the sorter he shouts out the name and invariably back someone comes with the information. On this particular morning a slightly incredulous voice raised above the usual hubbub said 'Mountain Ash'? and in the absence of any response I was able to help. Some little time later, rather to my surprise, another query was for Halesowen. Such wide-ranging familiarity with the location of towns and cities in the United Kingdom through the study of the railway system resulted in an above average report on my work during training.

After compiling this album of photographs with the indispensable aid of two publications — *Passengers No More* and *Pre-Grouping Atlas and Gazeteer*, both published by Ian Allan Ltd — this fund of knowledge has greatly increased; the reader, I trust will benefit similarly. *Rail Atlas of Britain 1977* (Oxford Publishing Company) also proved a most useful source of reference.

In conclusion I wish to record my thanks to C. R. L. Coles; L. Elsey; D. M. C. Hepburne-Scott; Lens of Sutton; R. A. Lissenden; P. J. Lynch and Brian Morrison for so promptly and willingly supplying or assisting in tracing many of the photographs. My thanks also to the publisher for allowing me the freedom of the files. Happy nostalgic wanderings!

Carshalton
Surrey

S. Creer
June 1978

Above: Boat of Garten-Craigellachie goods west of Nethy Bridge in the charge of Class 3F 0-6-0 No 57597, McIntosh's standard goods design for the Caledonian Railway. Boat of Garten still sees rail activity in that it is the headquarters of the Strathspey Railway, one of the many railway preservation schemes now flourishing in the UK. Photographed in September 1959. / *D. M. C. Hepburne-Scott*

Below: Class 2P 4-4-0 No 40617 bowls along near Auchindachy with the Elgin-Keith freight in May 1958. Ten years were to elapse before this route was closed. / *D. M. C. Hepburne-Scott*

Above: A contrast in motive power on the Elgin-Keith freight. Class D40 4-4-0 No 62264 leaves Dufftown in September 1955. / *D. M. C. Hepburne-Scott*

Below: Ex-LMS rolling stock forms a Perth-Edinburgh stopper on Glenfarg incline in September 1958, headed by Class 5MT 4-6-0 No 44977. This main line service ceased in January 1970. / *D. M. C. Hepburne-Scott*

Above: Another Perth-Edinburgh train, this time an LNER formation and express headlamps, all out on Glenfarg bank. Class V2 2-6-2 No 60958 is in charge. / *D. M. C. Hepburne-Scott*

Below: Photographed near Bucksburn in June 1954 is Class K2/2 2-6-0 No 61790 *Loch Lomond* heading a cattle train from Keith to Aberdeen.. / *D. M. C. Hepburne-Scott*

Above left: Push and pull fitted Class C15 4-4-2T No 67474 flaunting Class A lamps is seen at Arrochar on arrival from Craigendoran in July 1958. / *D. M. C. Hepburne-Scott*

Left: The morning goods from Fort William to Mallaig at Lochailort in October 1959. Class K2/2 2-6-0 No 61794 *Loch Oich* heads the train. / *D. M. C. Hepburne-Scott*

Above: Class D34 4-4-0 No 62467 *Glenfinnan* working the Thornton Junction-Leuchars Junction service arrives at Anstruther in September 1958. This route via Crail was closed in January 1969. / *D. M. C. Hepburne-Scott*

Above: Class D11/2 4-4-0 No 62678 *Luckie Mucklebakit* leaves Anstruther for Thornton Junction in September 1958. / *D. M. C. Hepburne-Scott*

Below: The early morning mixed train from Mallaig to Fort William would appear to cater more for the merchandise than the passenger. It is photographed near Mallaig Junction headed by Class K1 2-6-0 No 62031 in March 1959. / *D. M. C. Hepburne-Scott*

Above: The 10.00 Glasgow Queen Street-Fort William train nears journey's end in October 1959 with Class 5MT 4-6-0 No 44968 piloting Class K2/2 2-6-0 No 61784. / *D. M. C. Hepburne-Scott*

Below: Residents of the border town of North Berwick must surely be thankful they are still connected by this former North British branch to the East Coast main line. The 1977/78 timetable showed six up and five down trains Monday to Friday, with extra services on Saturdays and in the holiday months, ensuring a useful link with the Scottish capital. Class V2 2-6-2T No 67609 is seen before departure for Edinburgh Waverley in July 1953. / *P. H. Wells*

Above: Reedsmouth, on the Border Counties line, where Class J21 0-6-0 No 65061 is caught by the camera having a siesta with the empty stock of a special in connection with an agricultural show at Bellingham on the Waverley route on 22 September 1956. The lines to Riccarton Junction from Hexham and from Reedsmouth to Morpeth were closed on 15 October 1956 and 15 September 1952 respectively. / *I. S. Carr*

Below: Strictly speaking not a cross-country train but certainly a cross country route. The 10.05 Edinburgh Waverley-St Pancras, the 'Waverley' is seen near Falahill summit on the former NB line to Carlisle crossing wild and remote landscape; after closure in January 1969 the line became the object of a grandiose preservation scheme that never came to fruition and had no hope of so doing. Class A3 4-6-2 No 60099 *Call Boy*, now fitted with Kylchap blast pipe and double chimney, heads the train and probably came off at Carlisle. Photographed in September 1959. / *D. M. C. Hepburne-Scott*

Above: One of the earliest lines to be authorised in this country was the Newcastle & Carlisle Railway, sanctioned as far back as 1829. The through route, forging its way along the defile between the lofty and rugged border country and the mountains to the south, was ready for traffic by 1830. Here seen, westbound with freight passing Mickley, near Stocksfield, is Class K1 2-6-0 No 62027 in July 1955. / *J. D. Smith*

Below: Class V2 2-6-2 No 60812 arrives at Hexham westbound from Newcastle to Carlisle in August 1956. / *I. S. Carr*

Above: A Saturdays-only Carlisle-Newcastle train draws into Wetheral station, closed in January 1967, behind Fairburn Class 4 2-6-4T No 42094 in July 1955. / *R. Leslie*

Below: One of Gresley's rebuilds of the North Eastern Railway's Class D 4-4-4Ts, Class A8 4-6-2T No 69854 makes its way out of Whitby past Bog Hall box with the 17.55 to Middlesbrough via Battersby. In the right background can be seen the ruins of Whitby Abbey. / *A. M. Ross*

Above: A stunningly resplendent Class D49/1 4-4-0 No 62724 *Bedfordshire* moves away from Londesborough Road station, Scarborough, with the 10.00 to Manchester in August 1952. These excursion platforms have now been out of use for many years, the station being officially closed in 1966. / *K. Hoole*

Below: The scenic qualities of the North Yorkshire coast line and moors attracted frequent excursions from some inland centres of population; difficult terrain called for extra power, the climb at 1 in 39 to Ravenscar presenting a formidable obstacle. Standard Class 3 2-6-2T No 82027 piloting Class B1 4-6-0 No 61049 storm out of Fyling Hall and attack Ravenscar bank with a Bradford scenic excursion on 16 August 1959. / *D. Hardy*

Above: Another scenic excursion from Leeds via Whitby to Scarborough tops Ravenscar bank and draws to a halt to detach the pilot, Standard Class 4 2-6-4T No 80119. The train engine is Class B1 4-6-0 No 61069. No longer can the delights of the area be enjoyed from the train. Photographed on 26 August 1956. / *J. W. Armstrong*

Below: Gresley Class J39/2 0-6-0 No 64916 climbs away from Hartlepool with a Middlesbrough-Newcastle train. Permanent way work on the coastal section required diversion via the Wellfield Junction line, at the time normally closed to passenger traffic. To Hesleden the gradient steepens to 1 in 50 and No 64916 is here seen working hard on the incline on 9 May 1954. / *O. Metcalfe*

Above: An interesting record of the Pickering-Seamer line, closed in June 1950. Class G5 0-4-4T No 67315 is seen on 7 August 1956 at Thornton Dale, then the eastward limit of the permanent way. / *M. Mitchell*

Below: One of the Class D49/2 4-4-0 locomotives fitted with Lentz cam poppet valves, No 62757 *The Burton*, is at Harpham Crossing near Burton Agnes with the 16.30 Scarborough-Hull in August 1957. / *M. Mitchell*

Above left: A reminder that British Rail was originally divided into five Regions is given by the station nameboard at Cattal with the distinctive tangerine background. After an uneasy separate existence the North Eastern Region was merged with the Eastern from January 1967. Passing the station with the 14.10 Harrogate-York is Class D49/2 4-4-0 No 62765 *The Goathland* in August 1957. / *M. Mitchell*

Centre left: Five of Stanier's Class 3 2-6-2Ts of 1935 were rebuilt with larger boilers and here the photographer catches one of the quintet, No 40148, passing Prince of Wales Colliery Signal Box with the 17.35 Leeds-Knottingley local just before entering Pontefract Monkhill Lancashire & Yorkshire station in September 1957. / *P. Cookson*

Below left: Always a welcome sight were the 'Patriot' class 4-6-0s and here seen looking very smart is No 45517 of Bank Hall heading the 10.30 Liverpool-Newcastle at Castleford Central in September 1958. / *P. Cookson*

Above: Hughes 2-6-0 No 42770 is seen near Cross Gates with a Bradford to Scarborough excursion in June 1957. Note the unusual flush sided tender without coal rails and the Gresley-built strengthening stock. / *B. K. B. Green*

Below: Church Fenton, and a freight from Teeside to South Yorkshire comes off the Wetherby line just north of the station headed by one of the WD class locomotives. After the Wetherby lines had been swept away in 1964 much displaced through traffic was routed via York though trains such as the one illustrated had begun to use this diversion some years earlier. Photographed in March 1959. / *M. Mitchell*

Above: Standard Class 3 2-6-2Ts Nos 82028 (pilot) and 82027 climb up to the West Coast main line at Eden Valley Junction with the 08.50 Saltburn-Penrith train on a Sunday in August 1957. Presumably this was an excursion to the Lake District. / *R. Leslie*

Below: Ivatt Class 2 2-6-0 No 46470 pilots Class 4 2-6-0 No 43050 on the 11.00 Blackpool-South Shields train in August 1957. It is approaching Kirkby Stephen East on the Stainmore line, now alas, no more. / *R. Leslie*

Above: The summer 11.20 Blackpool-Newcastle express attained some popularity with the railway photographic fraternity; it was always double-headed and it traversed a very photogenic stretch of line crossing those two awesome and stately viaducts, Beulah and Deepdale. Standard Class 3 2-6-0s Nos 77012 and 77013 pass Ravenstonedale on the line from Tebay. Note the pilot engine, No 77012, sports a slip coupling. Photographed in September 1954. / J. W. Armstrong

Below: Compound Class 4P 4-4-0 No 41094 gets a clear road through Skipton station with a 10-coach excursion from Bradford to Morecambe travelling via Shipley and Keighley in April 1957. / C. P. Boocock

Above: A 'Jubilee' class 4-6-0 No 45589 *Gwalior* negotiates Skipton North Junction with the 09.40 Morecambe-Leeds in August 1951. The lines leading out of the photograph to the left were to Burnley and Blackburn via Colne. The latter town is now a terminus, services between it and Skipton having been withdrawn in February 1970. It is pleasant to recall the splendid 'swan song' of the class when, in 1967, aided and abetted by an enthusiastic shed staff at Holbeck, the summer Saturdays 06.40 Birmingham-Glasgow was a regular turn for them between Leeds and Carlisle. / *C. W. Bendall*

Below: The branch to Barnoldswick which left the Skipton-Colne line at Earby finally closed in August 1965. Here seen at Skipton in June 1952 is ex-L&Y 2-4-2T No 50621 of Manningham shed with the branch train. This photograph is of special interest as the locomotive is preserved and restored as L&Y No 1008 (Horwich Works No 1) and rests in the National Railway Museum at York. / *Harold D. Bowtell*

Above right: A Compound Class 4P 4-4-0 leaves Caton station on the Wennington Junction-Morecambe Promenade line in September 1958 with a Leeds City-Lancaster Green Ayre stopping train. The station was closed in May 1961 and closure of the line followed in January 1966. / *D. M. C. Hepburne-Scott*

Centre right: Beautifully turned out in the green livery lined in orange and black is 'Jubilee' class 4-6-0 No 45701 *Conqueror* heading a heavy Raleigh works outing special from Nottingham to Morecambe near Morecambe South Junction on 24 May 1952. / *E. D. Bruton*

Below right: After the slaughter of rail services in Lincolnshire only two coast resorts remained rail connected, Cleethorpes and Skegness; the latter was left with a tenuous link indeed and has since had cuts in its service resulting from some trains terminating at Boston during the winter months. Former Great Northern Class C12 4-4-2T No 67384 is leaving Sutton-on-Sea for Louth, the latter town still served by rail for freight only from Grimsby. Photographed in September 1954. / *E. C. Haywood*

Above: A 'Ragtimer' crosses the River Witham at Grand Sluice, Boston, with a Nottingham-Skegness excursion. The locomotive is Class K2/2 2-6-0 No 61763. Photographed in June 1952. / *L. Perrin*

Above right: On another closed line in Lincolnshire Class B1 4-6-0 No 61063 is passing Stickney on the loop line from Woodhall Junction to Bellwater Junction with an excursion from Chesterfield to Skegness in May 1950. The section from Bellwater Junction to Lincoln Central was axed in October 1970. / *W. A. Camwell*

Right: Class V2 2-6-2 No 60830 leaves Lincoln Central with the through Colchester-Newcastle train, now discontinued. Photographed in March 1956. / *Ian Allan Library*

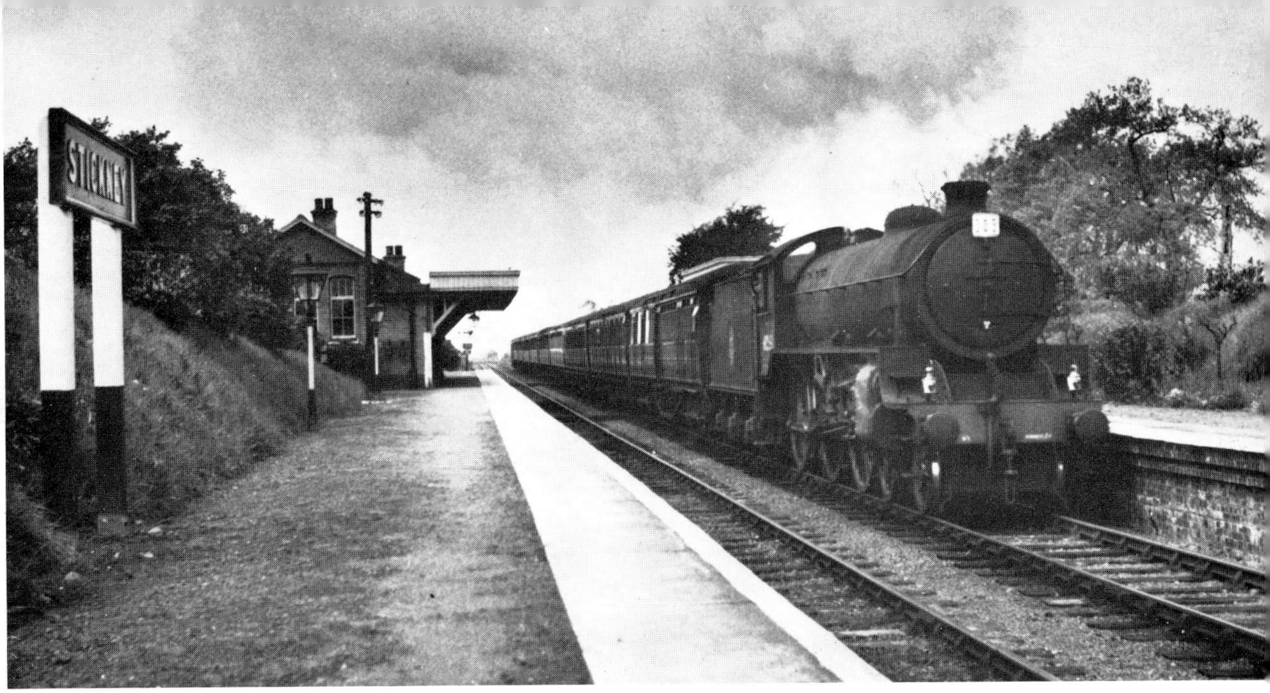
STICKNEY

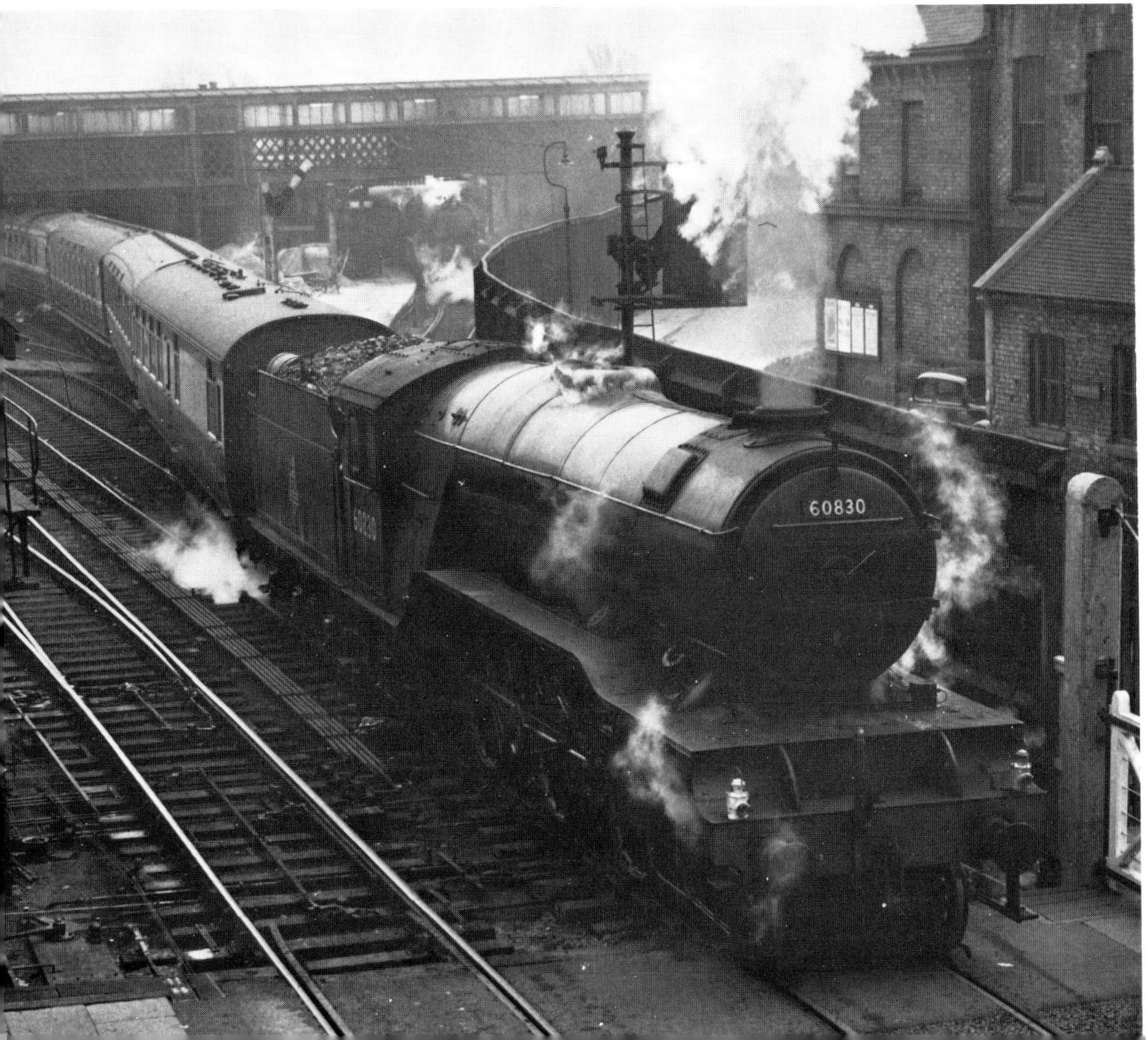
60830

Above: Ex-GC Class A5/1 4-6-2T No 69823 checks for the Rose Hill (Marple) stop in September 1956 with a Manchester London Road-Macclesfield local. This is now the end of the line from Marple Wharf Junction on the Manchester-New Mills line, the route from Rose Hill to Macclesfield having been closed in January 1970. / *T. Lewis*

Below: One of the 'Large Directors', Class D11/1 4-4-0 No 62661 *Gerard Powys Dewhurst*, approaches Northwich with the 16.40 from Manchester Central in May 1955. Note the contrasting semaphore signal styles, those on the left being of Cheshire Lines Committee origin. / *R. K. Evans*

Above: Class B1 4-6-0 No 61016 *Inyala* is seen at Todmorden in the Calder Valley with the Manchester-York express in September 1956. / *P. H. Wells*

Below: A rather grimy compound Class 4P 4-4-0 No 40910 heads a Manchester-Southport excursion near Glazebrook. / *P. Ransome-Wallis*

Above: Fowler Class 4 2-6-4T No 42393 is seen at Chester Northgate (now closed) with the 12.42 to Manchester Central in May 1959. / *S. D. Wainwright*

Below: The Great Central is not immediately associated with North Wales and Cheshire, particularly the area known as the Wirral peninsula, but so it was through its protégé the CLC. Doubtless many readers will be familiar with the complicated early railway history of these parts, culminating in the GCR taking control of the Wrexham, Mold & Connah's Quay Railway. Class N5 0-6-2T No 69281 is seen at Cefn-y-Bedd in March 1956 with a Hawarden Bridge-Wrexham local. Surprisingly the line is still in business. / *N. R. Knight*

Above right: Seacombe was the terminus of the short branch of the Wirral Railway from the junction at Bidston and it did not rate high in the estimation of the London Midland Region when plans were afoot to modernise the system in the area. It was excluded from the electrification of 1938 and closed when dmu operation was introduced. Class N5 0-6-2T No 69340 is about to leave Seacombe with a Wrexham train in March 1956. The clock tower on the skyline marks the entrance to one of the famous River Mersey ferries, in this case the Wallasey Corporation undertaking, the other being that of the Birkenhead authorities. / *Stanley Creer*

Centre right: Standard Class 3 2-6-2T No 82020 leaves Wrexham Exchange with the 11.25 Wrexham Central-Seacombe, providing a piquant contrast to the N5 0-6-2T, the more so in wearing a smart green lined out livery. Photographed in August 1958. / *T. Lewis*

Below right: Standard Class 5 4-6-0 No 73170 heads a relief to the 08.30 Bradford Exchange-Skegness train on the Great Northern & Great Eastern Joint line at Black Carr in August 1957. The overbridge carries the Dearne Valley Line which joins the up Joint line at Bessacarr Junction. / *Roy E. Vincent*

Above: A 'Claud' on the Midland. Class D16/3 4-4-0 No 62613 approaches Ketton & Collyweston with a Saturdays Only Hunstanton-Leicester train in July 1959. / *P. H. Wells*

Below: A memory of the M&GNJR. The location is Tydd, south of Sutton Bridge Junction, with Ivatt Class 4 2-6-0 No 43094 crossing the single-track bridge with the 11.50 from Kings Lynn to Peterborough in October 1958. / *Frank Church*

Above right: Class A5 4-6-2T No 69826 is hard put to it heading 11 corridors at Needham Junction. The train is the 06.24 from Derby Friargate to Yarmouth Vauxhall via Spalding and March. Interesting vintage vehicles are the first and third coaches that appear to be of GE and GC origin respectively. Photographed in September 1956. / *Dr Ian C. Allen*

Below right: The 10.15 from Norwich Thorpe to Lowestoft headed by Class K3/2 2-6-0 No 61926 approaches Reedham in April 1954. / *Roy E. Vincent*

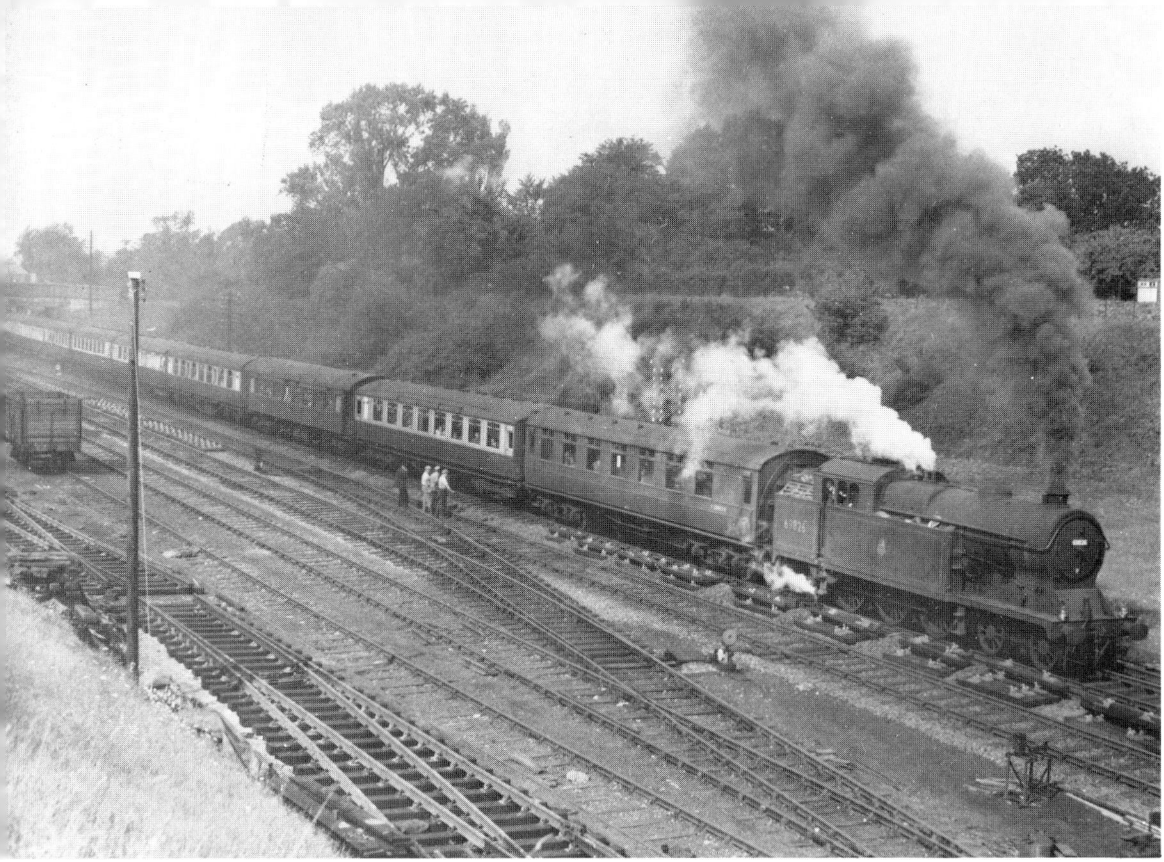

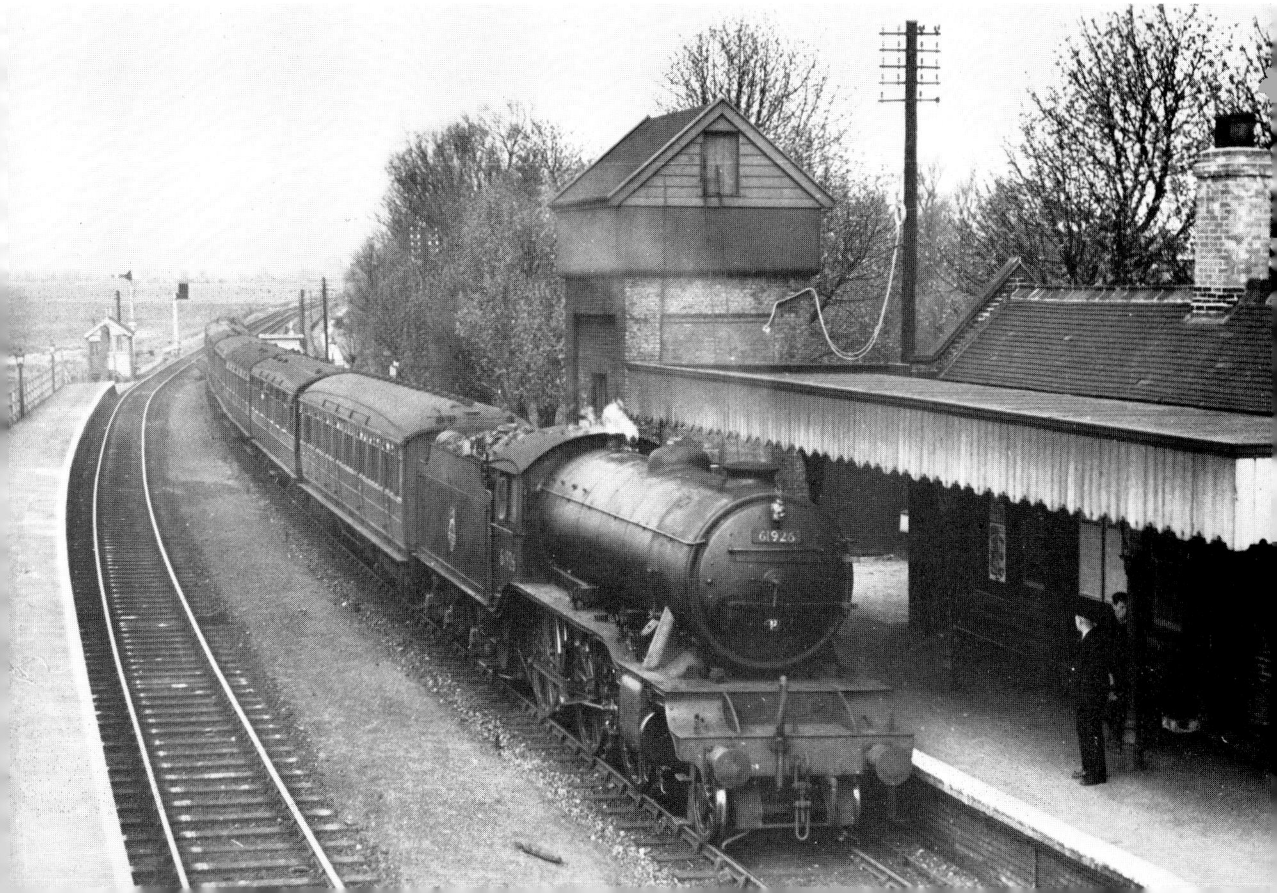

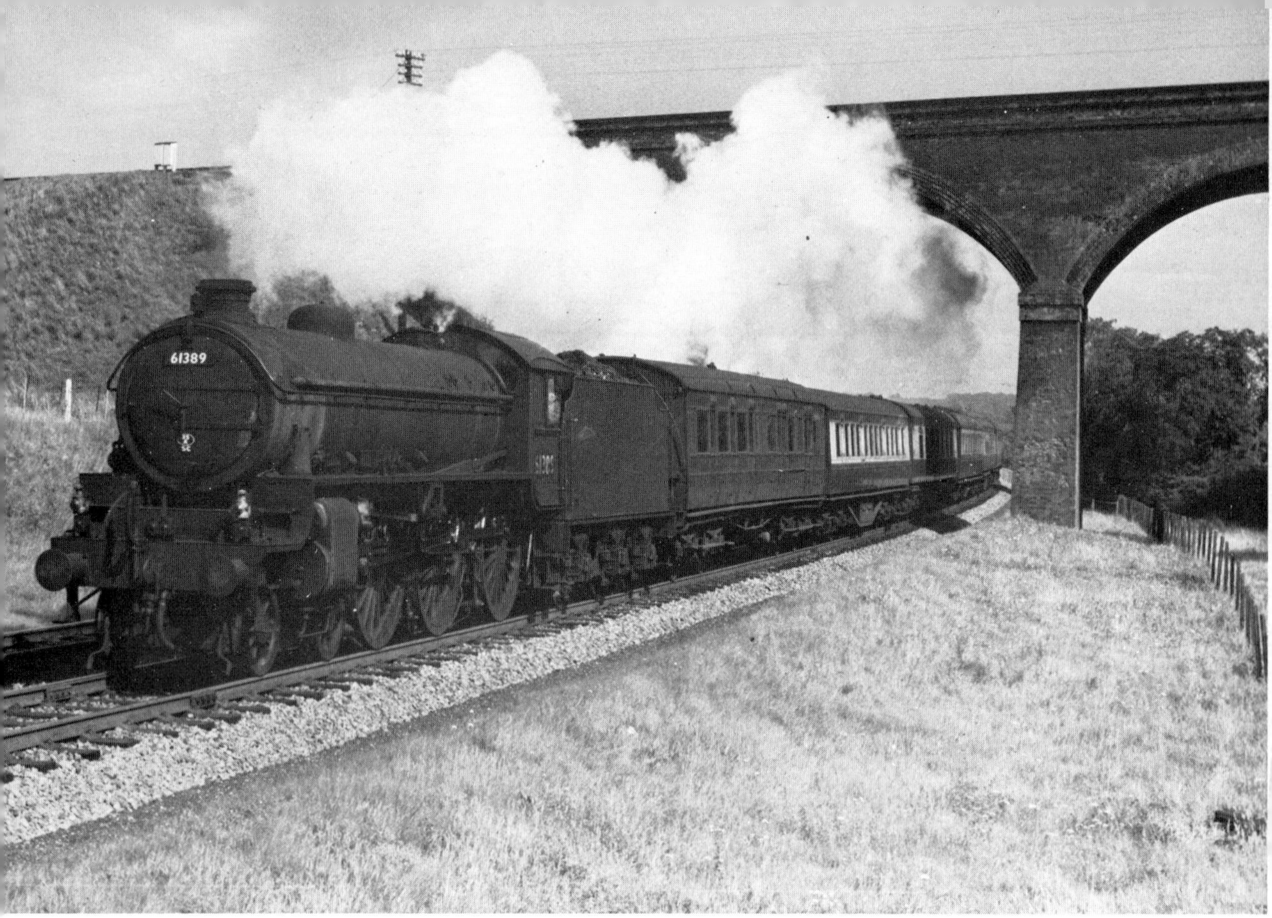
61389

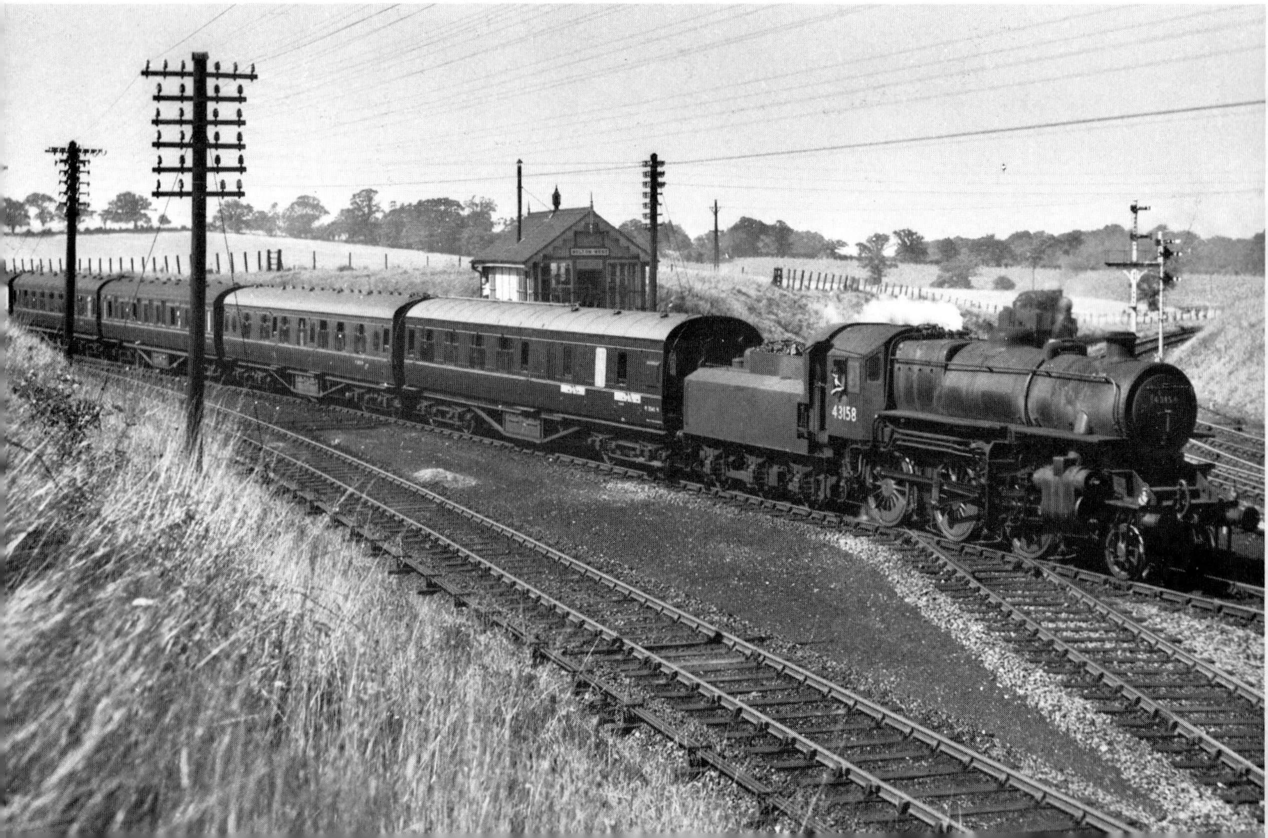
43158

Left: Despite an unkempt appearance Class B1 4-6-0 No 61389 seems in fine fettle as it sweeps along at Hartford Bridge near Norwich with the 12.13 from Lowestoft to Rugby. The viaduct carries the Ipswich main line. Photographed in September 1954. / *Roy E. Vincent*

Below left: 30 August 1958, in the last year of services on the M&GNJR. The scene is the west end of Melton Constable and shows Ivatt Class 4 2-6-0 No 43158 arriving with the 09.33 Derby Midland-Yarmouth. By this time nearly all workings were in the hands of this class. A sister engine stands beyond on the Cromer branch. / *G. R. Mortimer*

Right: Leaving Colchester is Class E4 2-4-0 No 62789 with the 15.44 Saturdays Only to Cambridge on 13 July 1957. / *G. R. Mortimer*

Below: Saffron Walden station with Class N7/3 0-6-2T No 69690 arriving with an afternoon train from Audley End to Bartlow. This line, one of a number selected by the Eastern Region for railbus operation was still unable to survive and closed in September 1964. Photographed on 16 June 1958. / *Frank Church*

Above left: At an unidentified location in Norfolk a 'Claud' heads a lightweight train from Yarmouth to Peterborough. The locomotive is Class D16/3 4-4-0 No 62515. Photographed in September 1955. / *Donald Kelk*

Centre left: Class B17/6 4-6-0 No 61658 *The Essex Regiment* speeds across the fens near Stonea with a York-Yarmouth express in May 1954. / *T. B. Paisley*

Below left: Class B12/3 4-6-0 No 61561 takes the single line out of Long Melford with the 08.14 summer Saturdays Leicester-Clacton-on-Sea after waiting in the station loop for the opposite service to pass. Photographed in July 1958. / *G. R. Mortimer*

Above: A scene on the erstwhile Bishops Stortford-Braintree link, closed in March 1952. Class J20/1 0-6-0 No 64696 is hauling a train consisting of empty trucks mostly used for sugar beet traffic to Felstead factory and is leaving Takeley station. In pleasant contrast is the other line out of Braintree, to Witham on the GE main line, which not only still thrives but is now electrified and includes a few through trains to London. / *R. E. S. Thurgood*

Below: Class B17/6 4-6-0 No 61651 *Derby County* is leaving the GE main line at Marks Tey with one of the German-built railbuses in tow, presumably en route to the Cambridge area where the Mildenhall and Saffron Walden branches were to be the first to be tried out with these vehicles. Photographed in March 1958. / *M. Mensing*

Above: Class B12/3 4-6-0 No 61577 leaves Haughley with a Bury St Edmunds to Ipswich train in April 1952. In common with many GE section branch line and secondary services the formation contains a liberal sprinkling of pre-Grouping coaches including a former NER clerestory. The station was closed in January 1967. / *P. J. Lynch*

Below: An unidentified Class J15 0-6-0 heads the 11.52 train from Marks Tey to Cambridge and approaches Sudbury Goods signalbox in March 1954. Sudbury is now the terminus of the line from Marks Tey, the line north through Long Melford to Cambridge having been closed as far as Shelford in March 1967. / *Roy E. Vincent*

Above: Ivatt Class 2 2-6-0 No 46404 makes a spirited departure from Huntingdon East with the afternoon train to Cambridge in March 1954, a service withdrawn in September 1959. / *E. H. Sawford*

Below: The Standard version of the Class 2 2-6-0, here represented by No 78021, is also on the Huntingdon-Cambridge line and seen approaching Godmanchester with a Cambridge train. The photographer notes that this may be a through train from Kettering, a reminder that the Midland Railway had running powers over this section. Photographed in May 1959. / *D. M. C. Hepburne-Scott*

Above: Class B17/6 4-6-0 No 61645 *The Suffolk Regiment* at Fordham Junction with the roundabout Peterborough-Cambridge via Newmarket train. The German-built railbus at the platform was on trial on the Mildenhall branch. Photographed in May 1958. / *D. Penney*

Below: What appears to be a case of borrowing gave the photographer an unusual shot at Wellington (Salop) in July 1954 when Standard Class 6 4-6-2 No 72008 *Clan Macleod* of Carlisle was caught on a three-coach stopping train from Shrewsbury to Stafford. / *B. Sackville*

Above: On a line closed in March 1962 former MR 0-4-4T No 58091 is seen at Olney in June 1950 with the Northampton-Bedford auto train. / *W. A. Camwell*

Below: On 3 August 1957 a relief to the Newcastle-Bournemouth train was run from York. The photograph is of exceptional interest in that the locomotive, Stanier Class 8F 2-8-0 No 48536, headed the train throughout, surely one of the longest, if not the longest journey a member of the class ever made hauling a passenger train. The comments of the crew concerned would no doubt have been illuminating on arrival at Bournemouth. The train is seen approaching Rugby Central. / *Rev A. W. V. Mace*

Above: Another nostalgic scene never to be captured again shows Peterborough East, which was closed together with the line to Rugby in June 1966. On the left is Class 4F 0-6-0 No 44519 before departure with the 15.45 Northampton train. Class C12 4-4-2T No 67368 is on the right acting as station pilot. A preserved line, the Nene Valley Railway, now occupies the section of the Peterborough-Rugby line between Orton Mere and Wansford. Photographed in Apirl 1954. / *J. P. Wilson*

Below: A cross-country idyll as Stanier Class 2P 0-4-4T No 41902 pauses at Daventry with the Northampton-Leamington local. The line was closed in August 1958. / *A. E. Davies*

Above: Class B1 4 6-0 No 61095 trails a self-weighing tender and some assorted rolling stock over and above the three corridors for clients as it leaves Clifton Mill station with the 07.05 Peterborough East-Rugby Midland train. / *A. E. Davies*

Below: Class D11/1 4-4-0 No 62666 *Zeebrugge* from Lincoln is seen near Carlton & Netherfield with the 13.58 Nottingham Midland to Lincoln St Marks in September 1956. The 1950s saw a variety of 4-4-0s on this former Midland line, ex-MR and LMS 2Ps and Compounds which were in turn supplanted by rebuilt 'Clauds'. / *P. J. Lynch*

Above: Leaving Manton Tunnel in June 1959 is Class 2P 4-4-0 No 40452 heading a Peterborough-Leicester local on a line it is pleasant to note has not been closed. / *J. L.Boyd*

Below: Another ex-MR Johnson 0-4-4T No 58056 stands at Southwell with the branch train to Rolleston Junction in August 1954. The line was closed in June 1959 and originally the route continued west from Southwell to Mansfield, from which section services were withdrawn as far back as August 1929. / *P. J. Lynch*

Above: Bank Holidays are always occasions for extra workings and Class 4F 0-6-0 No 44064 is seen approaching Hillmorton, Rugby, on the Northampton line with empty stock on Whit Monday 26 May 1958. / *M. Mensing*

Below: An eastbound coal train from Colwick crosses the River Trent on Radcliffe viaduct hauled by Class WD 2-8-0 No 90000 in July 1955. / *J. F. Oxley*

Above: A work-stained GN Class J6 0-6-0 No 64249 stands at Basford North station on the 19.15 from Grantham to Derby Friargate. The section from Basford North to Netherfield & Colwick was closed in April 1960. Photographed in July 1959. / *P. J. Lynch*

Below: An unidentified Standard Class 2 2-6-0 approaches Borth with a Shrewsbury-Aberystwyth stopping train in July 1957. / *Stanley Creer*

Above: A pre-Grouping veteran of the Cambrian Railway still at work in May 1950 — 0-6-0 No 896. Starting life in April 1908, three years from the date of this photograph were to pass before withdrawal in 1953. The bucolic air of lonely Moat Lane Junction, closed with the line to Brecon in December 1962, is well brought out in this photograph of the three-coach train to Llanidloes. Departure was duly made still with the light engine headcode in place!
/ *P. J. Lynch*

Below: 'Castle' class 4-6-0 No 5032 *Usk Castle* on a West to North express (originating at Plymouth North Road) passes Marsh Brook, south of Church Stretton on the Shrewsbury-Hereford line, in July 1951. / *C. R. L. Coles*

Above: Two Fowler Class 4 2-6-4Ts Nos 42385 and 42305 stand at Craven Arms with a five-coach Shrewsbury-Swansea High Street train before tackling the rigours of the 90-mile run over the Central Wales line to Llanelli, which includes the climb to Sugar Loaf summit, 820ft above sea level. In recent years rationalisation of this former LNWR route has been undertaken on a large scale in an endeavour to make it solvent; this has included introduction of a 30-mile single line block section from Craven Arms to Llandrindod Wells, a counter-productive measure as it plays havoc at times with punctual running. Not envisaged in the basic rail network plan, the line is exceptionally favoured in its survival. Note the train engine still carries the initials LMS at this date, July 1951. / *C. R. L. Coles*

Below: GW 7400 class 0-6-0PT No 7402 stands in Llandilo station on the Central Wales line during a spell of duty on the Llandilo-Carmarthen service which ceased with the closure of the line from Llandilo to Abergwili Junction in September 1963. / *Lens of Sutton*

Above right: The second part of the through Hastings-Walsall train leaves Birmingham New Street in August 1958 with Standard Class 4 2-6-4T No 80038 piloting Class 5MT 4-6-0 No 44840. The tank is a Watford engine and presumably worked through to Walsall, perhaps indicating that all was not well with the Class 5. / *M. Mensing*

Below right: Morning sunlight and shadow combine to make an attractive portrait of Class 5MT 4-6-0 No 44964 as the regulator is eased open and the 08.05 to Newcastle moves out of Birmingham New Street in June 1957. / *M. Mensing*

Above: Class 5MT 4-6-0 No 45379 passes Gamlingay on the Cambridge-Bedford line westbound with a special train. Services through to Oxford were withdrawn in January 1968. / *J. Spencer Gilks*

Below: Class D16/3 4-4-0 No 62574 from Cambridge crosses the East Coast main line at Sandy on an afternoon train from Oxford to Cambridge in May 1952. The lattice girder bridge was later replaced but the new structure had a very short spell of useful life, carrying the trains on this former LNWR cross-country route for only nine years. It was taken down in February 1976. / *P. J. Lynch*

Above: Standard Class 4 4-6-0 No 75037 is seen immediately south of Cambridge with an afternoon train to Bletchley in June 1959. / *D. M. C. Hepburne-Scott*

Above right: Stanier Class 4 2-6-4T No 42566 leaves the LNWR station at Brackley on the Verney Junction-Banbury Merton Street line with a Buckingham-Banbury train. Photographed in May 1951. / *P. H. Wells*

Right: A pleasant autumn afternoon at Buckingham sees Standard Class 2 2-6-2T No 84002 about to return to Bletchley in October 1956. This push-pull service was withdrawn in September 1964. / *Stanley Creer*

Above: A rare record is this photograph of the relatively unknown stretch of line between Banbury and the GC at Culworth Junction. It shows the 13.16 Banbury-Woodford between Chalcombe Road and Eydon Road platforms in July 1959 hauled by Class L1 2-6-4T No 67740. The line closed in September 1966. / *M. Mitchell*

Below: This album could not omit the Stratford-on-Avon & Midland Junction Railway, which ran from Broom on the MR line via Evesham to Ravenstone Wood Junction on the Bedford-Northampton line. A useful cross-country route for Bristol and South Wales freights, it was closed as a through link in March 1965, thereafter in various stages. Passing Byfield, and running on the connecting line from Woodford Halse, is WD class 2-8-0 No 90573 with the 19.20 Woodford-South Wales freight in June 1959. / *M. Mitchell*

Above: Class 4F 0-6-0 No 44524 labours uphill with a Stratford-on-Avon to Blisworth goods in June 1959. It is about to cross the GC main line immediately south of Woodford Halse. / *M. Mitchell*

Below: This lineside shot of the 08.30 Cardiff-Newcastle train throws into relief the abrupt change of gradient at the platform end at Bromsgrove station, at the foot of the Lickey incline. Class 2P 4-4-0 No 40601 is piloting Standard Class 5MT 4-6-0 No 73116 as they take the strain on the 1 in 37 bank. Speculation on how these two locomotives came to work this turn makes an interesting talking point. No 40601 is a Bath (Green Park) engine and the 4-6-0 hails from Nine Elms, Southern Region's London motive power for the Western Division. Photographed in July 1958. / *Stanley Creer*

BRITISH RAILWAYS
CLIFFORD SIDING
GOODS & COAL DEPOT

AYLESBURY
6167
BAR

Above left: Heyday of freight, to use the photographer's own words (though he omitted to include the date) on the S&MJR. It is possible that this scene was recorded in the decade covered by this album — the tail end of the 1950s perhaps? Too interesting a photograph not to be given the benefit of the doubt. Forming the parade is 'Hall' class 4-6-0 No 5990 *Dorford Hall*, an unidentified Stanier Class 8F 2-8-0, and Standard Class 9F 2-10-0 No 92246: the latter has just left the single line from Fenny Compton hauling a South Wales iron ore train. A good illustration of permissive block working here. / *John R. P. Hunt*

Below left: GW 6100 class 2-6-2T No 6167 is seen at Aylesbury after arrival with the 15.06 train from Maidenhead in April 1959. The closing of the section between Bourne End and High Wycombe in May 1970 put an end to this through route. / *M. Mitchell*

Above: Aylesbury was also served by the former LNWR branch from Cheddington on the West Coast main line. Class G2A 0-8-0 No 49144 is seen at the High Street terminus with the branch freight. As the date of the demise of steam on BR recedes ever further into the past it may be recalled, with some surprise, that the familiar outline of these LNWR 7Fs could still be seen trundling about in the early 1960s, final withdrawals occurring in 1964. The branch was closed in February 1953. / *C. R. L. Coles*

Right: The 10.35 Wolverhampton-Penzance express runs on to the Honeybourne-Cheltenham line (closed in March 1968) headed by 'Castle' class 4-6-0 No 5008 *Raglan Castle*. The tall signal gantry controls the junction of the Honeybourne and Stratford routes and the embankment in the background carries the main Paddington-Worcester via Oxford main line. Photographed in August 1951. / *J. C. Flemons*

Above: Unrecognisable today after track alteration and rationalisation is Cheltenham Lansdown Junction. Class 2P 4-4-0 No 40409 passes by on a Gloucester-Birmingham stopping train in May 1953. / *P. J. Lynch*

Below: A very smart turn out for a Cardiff-Birmingham train passing Cheltenham Lansdown Junction hauled by 'Hall' class 4-6-0 No 6918 *Sandon Hall* in April 1956 / *P. Ransome-Wallis*

Above: 'Hall' class 4-6-0 No 6903 *Belmont Hall* leaves Gloucester with the Cardiff portion of the Newcastle-Cardiff and Bristol train composed of ex-LNER stock in August 1952. / *F. C. Scoon*

Below: A Midland Class 3F 0-6-0 No 43258 works hard near Charfield on the ascent up to and through Wickwar Tunnel, which lies ahead, hauling freight from the Midlands to Bristol. Photographed in May 1952. / *P. M. Alexander*

Inset left: 'Jubilee' class 4-6-0 No 45682 *Trafalgar* moves away from Bristol Temple Meads with the 10.20 York-Newcastle express in July 1953. / *C. R. L. Coles*

Left: The GW magic comes over strongly in this fine shot of 'Hall' class 4-6-0 No 5980 *Dingley Hall* making light of five bogies up the 1 in 60 of Sapperton bank with the 14.10 Gloucester-Swindon stopper. In recent years the line has been singled from Kemble to Swindon. / *G. F. Heiron*

Below: Unidentified motive power heads north into the morning mist with the 07.35 Bristol-Bradford express. The train is pulling away from Mangotsfield station, then in business in May 1956. Installation of modern signalling and track improvements allied to the abandonment of other cross-country lines has assured the future of the NE/SW route. / *G. F. Heiron*

Above: A line-up at Bath of three Hughes/Fowler 2-6-0s Nos 42799, 42921 and 42782, waits to take expresses on to the North as they arrive from Bournemouth in August 1958. Nearly eight years were to elapse before the S&D succumbed to the inevitable, the closure mourned by enthusiasts everywhere no matter what their allegiance happened to be. / *Ivo Peters*

Below: Class 2P 4-4-0 No 40652 and Standard Class 5 4-6-0 No 73051 coast into Bath Junction off the 1 in 50 gradient with the northbound 'Pines Express' in June 1959. / *D. M. C. Hepburne-Scott*

Above right: On a line that received as much adulation as the GWR itself, a famous train to traverse its metals, the 'Pines Express', climbs the 1 in 50 between Evercreech Junction and Shepton Mallet on the S&D in April 1957. Class 2P 4-4-0 No 40569 pilots Standard Class 5 4-6-0 No 73047. / *C. P. Boocock*

Below right: 'Modified Hall' No 6988 *Swithland Hall* leaves Chippenham with a Weymouth to Wolverhampton train in August 1951. / *G. J. Jefferson*

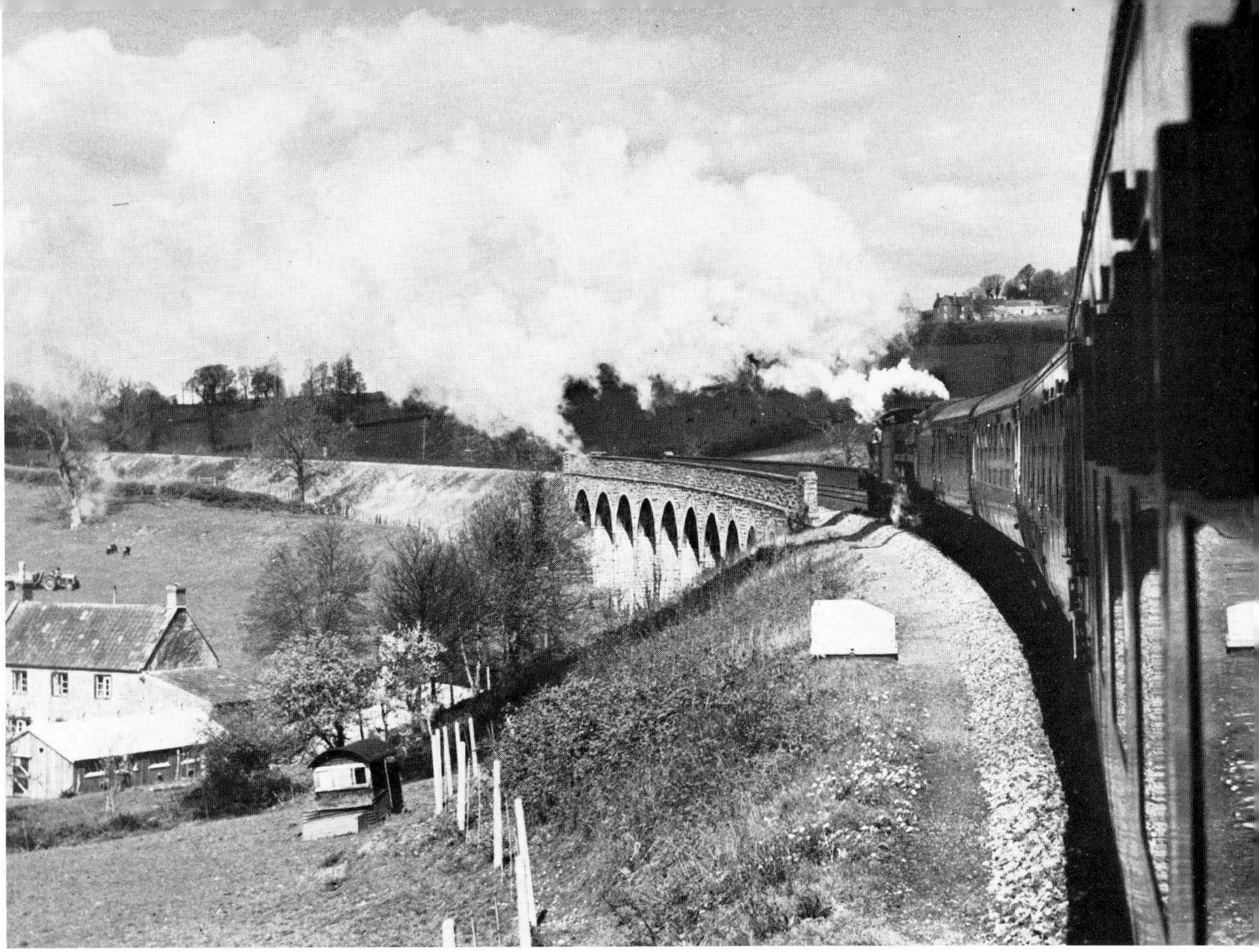

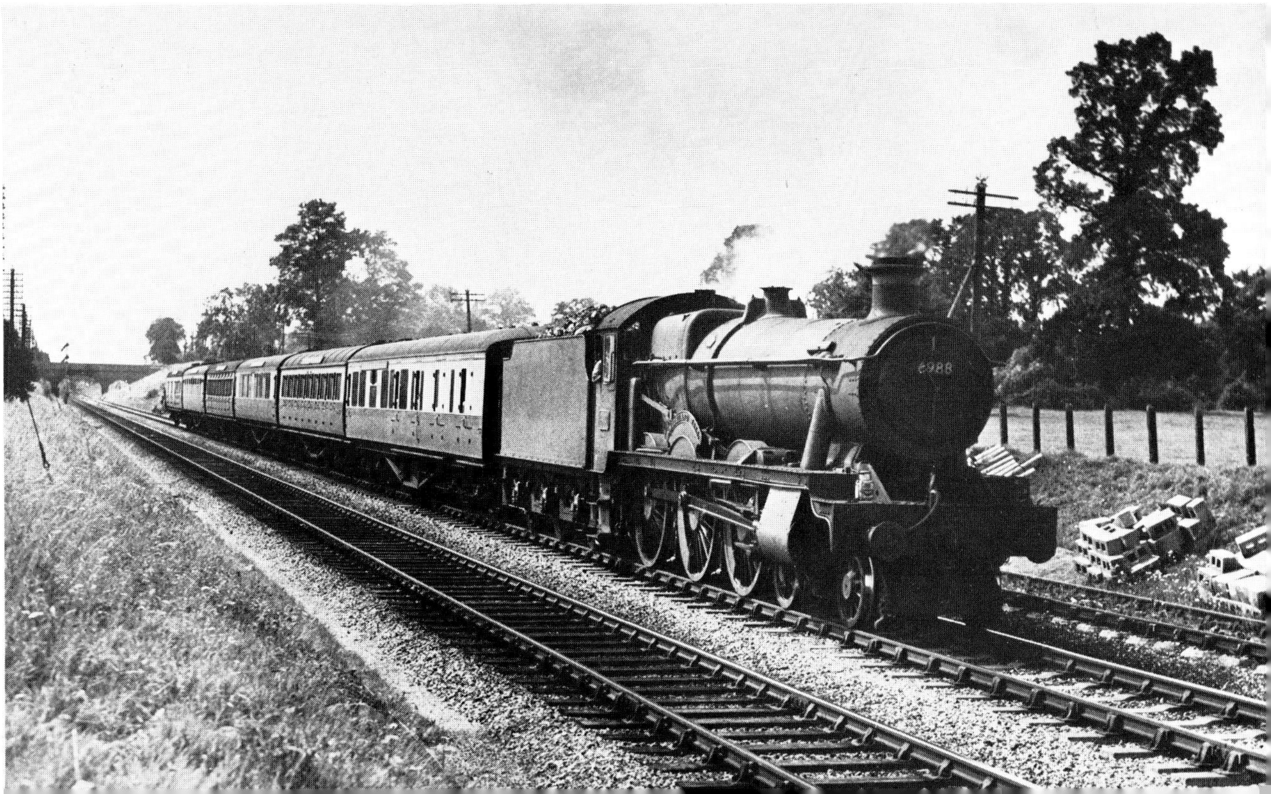

Above: Side lighting always enhances a photograph as again demonstrated in this shot of Collett 0-6-0 No 2245 approaching Hampstead Norris in April 1955 with the 16.20 local from Newbury to Didcot; the line closed in September 1962. What appears to be scratches in the sky are in reality vapour trails from aircraft, the pilots of which are having a field day on a beautiful spring afternoon. / *D. J. Beaver*

Below: 'West Country' class 4-6-2 No 34093 *Saunton* passes Didcot North Junction with the Bournemouth-Birkenhead train in August 1954. / *C. G. Pearson*

Above: Graceful Tilbury type 4-4-2T No 41944 stokes up at Southminster before departure for Wickford on the Liverpool St-Southend line in February 1954. / *P. J. Lynch*

Below: Ex-LNER Class J50/4 0-6-0T No 68989, one of the rebuilds from Class J50/3 to give a larger bunker, climbs out of Acton yard with a cattle train for East London. April 1955. / *B. Canning*

Above: A summer Ramsgate-Nottingham train at Kensington Olympia in August 1950. The locomotive, Class N 2-6-0 No 31816, has just uncoupled and is drawing ahead to make way for the Eastern Region engine that is taking over. / *Ian Allan Library*

Below: The York-Bournemouth express passes Reading West in July 1955 headed by a Class N15 4-6-0 No 30783 *Sir Gillemere*. The link between the Western and Southern Regions provided by the route to Basingstoke gained in stature when lines such as the S&D closed. During the summer months traffic is still intensive with all

the seasonal inter Regional excursions added to the regular through services. / *C. R. L. Coles*

Right: An impressive shot of 'Lord Nelson' class 4-6-0 No 30862 *Lord Collingwood* passing Reading West station with the 10.23 York-Bournemouth in April 1954. / *T. E. Williams*

Above: The Kent Coast portion of the through train from Birkenhead leaves Redhill behind 'Schools' class 4-4-0 No 30913 *Christ's Hospital* in April 1955. Note the GW stock, which was used on alternate days with Southern vehicles. / *Stanley Creer*

Below: The through train from the Kent and Sussex coasts to Birkenhead leaves Redhill hauled by Class U1 2-6-0 No 31896. The Dover and Hastings portions of this service joined up at this Surrey crossroads. The none too clean locomotive contrasts strongly with the freshly painted coaches finished in the experimental carmine and cream livery. This through service was withdrawn in 1963. Photographed in April 1955. / *Stanley Creer*

Above: Western Region's 'Manor' class 4-6-0s were a common enough sight on the Reading-Redhill line, sharing duties with the 4300 class and the Maunsell Moguls. On this occasion No 7813 *Freshford Manor* was working an unusual turn returning to Swindon the empty stock of a special that it had brought down earlier in the day. It is seen leaving Redhill in July 1957. / *Stanley Creer*

Below: A touch of Edwardian splendour was occasionally to be enjoyed on the cross-country line between Tonbridge and Reading, provided by Wainwright's Class D 4-4-0s. Here No 31574 was recorded at Reigate making a last stop before arriving at Redhill. The 2-BIL set on the left is the Reigate portion, detached at Redhill, of a London-Brighton train, a practice now discontinued for some years, a shuttle being operated instead. / *Ian Allan Library*

Above: Class H 0-4-4T No 31193 crosses the main line into Tonbridge as it arrives from Redhill. In 1950 traffic warranted a six-coach train (note the birdcage guard's lookout set). Today three bogies are more than sufficient for a line that has difficulty in maintaining passenger traffic. Photographed in September 1950. / *C. R. L. Coles*

Below: A Western Region excursion from Princes Risborough to Littlehampton eases through Dorking North station in the 1950s (year and month unrecorded) headed by 'Battle of Britain' class 4-6-2 No 34083 *605 Squadron*. It is just about to pass beneath the Redhill-Guildford line at Deepdene; inter-Regional excursions to the West Sussex resorts more often than not used the Brighton line, reaching the coast by the Preston Park spur to Hove. The Mid-Sussex line was taken less frequently, thus the passage of a steam-hauled passenger train through Dorking North was something of a rarity. / *Stanley Creer*

Above: Class C2X 0-6-0 No 32536 rolls the 09.02 Hove-Three Bridges freight near Horsham in May 1959. / *J. Scrace*

Below: Another shot of the through train to Birkenhead, hauled by commendably clean L class 4-4-0 No 31776 of Ashford. This is the Hastings portion on its way to Redhill where the Kent coast train is joined. An interesting Southern characteristic is headcode variations, the discs shown here indicating the Brighton-Redhill section; the train reversed at the former station, also at Eastbourne before that, followed by further manoeuvring at Redhill. Possibly such comings and goings played a part in the discontinuation of this cross-country service. The lines leading out of the photograph to the left are for Lewes and Eastbourne, leaving the main Brighton line here at Keymer Junction. August 1956. / *P. J. Lynch*

Above: 'West Country' class 4-6-2 No 34048 *Crediton* leaves
Chichester with the 11.00 Brighton-Cardiff train in March 1956.
Cross-country services from Brighton to South Wales and the West
were phased out but later a need was felt for some reinstatement and
a Saturdays Only service now operates to Exeter St David's.
/ *C. R. L. Coles*

Above right: Unofficially christened the 'Lancing Belle', the
workmen's train from Lancing to Brighton, hauled as usual by two
Class E4 0-6-2Ts, leaves Hove for Brighton on 4 May 1956. On this
day No 32566 pilots No 32481. / *W. M. J. Jackson*

Right: Steam has returned to rural Hampshire now that the Mid-
Hants preservation project (The Watercress Line) has got off the
ground operating from Ropley to Alresford. At the former station a
Class 700 0-6-0 No 30350 is arriving on the 08.20 Eastleigh-Alton
goods in June 1956. / *J. H. Aston*

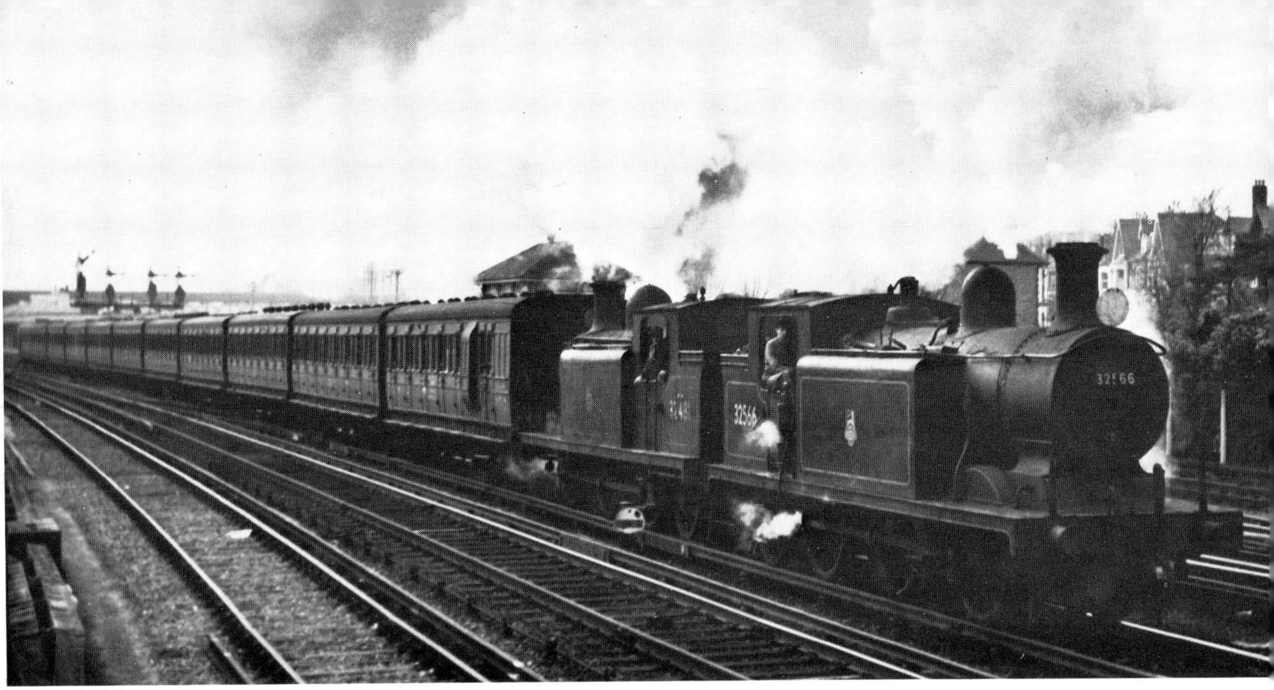
32566
32566

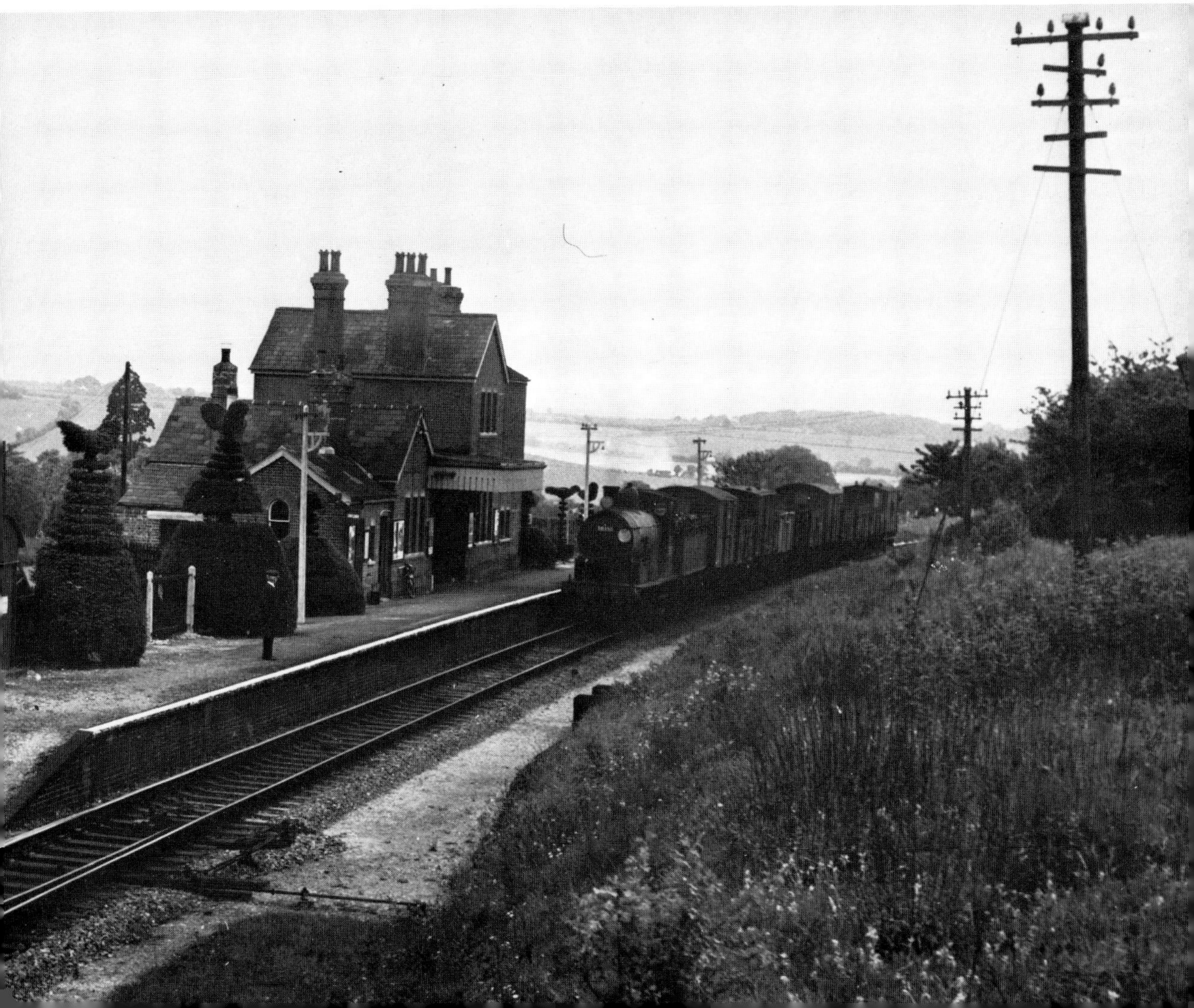

Above: A Portsmouth-Cardiff train leaves Salisbury in August 1958 hauled by 'Hall' class 4-6-0 No 4945 *Milligan Hall.* / *Stanley Creer*

Below: In May 1958 Class T9 4-4-0 No 30310 moves its three-coach train of empty stock away from Salisbury station, after completing the journey from Bournemouth via Wimborne, a cross country route that closed in May 1964. No 30310 is one of 15 out of the 66 engines that made up the class originally, with wider cabs and splashers and without coupling rod splashers. / *Stanley Creer*

Above: A Urie Class S15 4-6-0 No 30507 heads a Brighton-Salisbury freight round the curve from Eastleigh main to the Romsey line in July 1959. / *L. Elsey*

Below: Heading cross-country over the Didcot, Newbury & Southampton line from Winchester Chesil to Enborne Junction on the GW Berks & Hants line is 2251 class 0-6-0 No 3210, passing Northam Junction with a Southampton Central to Didcot stopping train. This cross-country route was closed down in March 1960. Photographed in July 1951. / *L. Elsey*

Above: The Midland & South Western Junction line from Andoversford Junction (near Cheltenham) on the Western Region to Red Post Junction, west of Andover Junction on the Southern Region, was closed to passengers in September 1961. On a bleak December day in 1950, 4300 class 2-6-0 No 6309 nears the end of its journey overland from Cheltenham to Southampton Terminus. The weather conditions draw attention to the skimpy cab so long a feature of earlier GW locomotives; as can be seen, the engine crew is not completely protected from whatever comes from above. / *L. Elsey*

Below: Class N15 4-6-0 No 30795 *Sir Dinadan* is seen between Eastleigh and Chandlers Ford with a heavy van train from Portsmouth Harbour to Salisbury in April 1956. / *L. Elsey*

Above: 'Grange' class 4-6-0 No 6866 *Morfa Grange* heads a
Birmingham to Portsmouth Harbour train near Eastleigh South in
July 1954. / *L. Elsey*

Below: Maunsell Class Q 0-6-0 No 30530 photographed between
Eastleigh and Botley with an Eastleigh to Portsmouth stopping train
in May 1956. / *L. Elsey*

Above: Southern enthusiasts resident in Hampshire must have been greatly pleased when the Brighton Atlantics were doing a stint on the Brighton-Bournemouth trains in the 1950s and here seen leaving Southampton in August 1952 is Class H2 4-4-2 No 32421 *South Foreland.* / L. Elsey

Below: No 32424 *Beachy Head* is leaving Christchurch with the Brighton-Bournemouth train in May 1954. / D. M. C. Hepburne-Scott

Above: One of the Brighton's best designs, the K class 2-6-0 was equally at home on freight or passenger duties. No 32337 ambles along the single line from Knowle to Fareham with the morning Salisbury-Fratton goods in March 1958. / *D. F. Fereday Glenn*

Below: 'West Country' class 4-6-2 No 34110 *66 Squadron* hauling an Exeter Central-Weymouth excursion, traverses the wartime connection from the LSW to the GW line at Yeovil South Junction. At Yeovil Pen Mill the train will reverse; many such connections were laid down in various parts of the country to assist in the speeding up of military specials, many naturally being of an inter-Regional nature. All were put in at Government expense and did not become railway property. Most have since been dismantled though the Yeovil connection remains in use for freight. Photographed in August 1959. / *S. C. Nash*

Above: The 15.30 Weymouth to Maiden Newton train leaves Weymouth in June 1959 behind GW 1400 class 0-4-2T No 1453. / *S. Rickard*

Below: 'Hall' class 4-6-0 No 5978 *Bodinnick Hall* arrives at Maiden Newton in March 1958 with a Weymouth to Yeovil stopping train as 4500 class 2-6-2T No 4507 waits in the bay with the connection for the Bridport branch, now closed, though it did manage to survive until May 1975. / *C. P. Boocock*